REDEEMED

Jesus Is The Key

Tammy J. Glenn

ISBN: 1986387410
ISBN 13: 9781986387415

CONTENTS

Dedicated to my husband, Rusty Glenn—you are my rock; my daughter, Brooke Kingsley, who is my treasure from God; and my brother Zane Palmer, who is one of the strongest but gentlest people I know—you have a heart of love.

ACKNOWLEDGEMENTS

I wanted to thank some people in my life who have encouraged me while writing this book, prayed for me, believed in me, or simply walked with me on this great journey we are on with Jesus.

My husband, who has been my prayer warrior over me and has stood by my side through so many ups and downs. Your prayers have been like a blanket covering me. I love you.

My daughter, who will always be my Boog, you are one of the most encouraging people I know. As I have watched you grow and become a mother yourself, you have amazed me with the strength and love you have. I thank God for your gift of encouragement because it is contagious! You are going to do great things for God!

My mama, Judy Tomlinson, who absolutely loved to hear my stories about God! Her enthusiasm made me believe that others may actually like to read them. Mom, your gift of laughter will ring in my ears forever!

My brother Zane Palmer. Your love for people and desire to help and give to others is a gift from God! I thank God he made you my brother! May your heart always stay soft.

My cousin Lori Arthur. You are the light that shines in darkness! Your love for God is what made me turn to look at Jesus. Your gift to make people laugh has brought me out of some of the deepest pits. I thank God, we are cousins and now sisters in Christ!

My uncle Dale Mathias, for standing firm in your faith for Jesus! I will forever remember you walking me to the front of that church to give my life to Jesus!

My friend of thirty-five years, Sheila Lester. So many times I wanted to give up feeling so unworthy to tell these stories, but there you were lifting me up. You are my sister sent from heaven! Thank you for always being there for me my friend!

My friend Mary Jo Hedberg, whom I call MJ. You are a prayer warrior! I thank God that He brought you into my life to teach me!

My aunt Betty Mathias. Every time I have needed prayer for myself or others, you have been there! You are a mighty prayer warrior!

My friend Nicole Cooper, who is like a daughter to me! Your perseverance and ability to lean on God through some very tough times is a confirmation of how mighty and powerful the God we serve is! God is doing great things in your life!

My son in-law, Jordan Kingsley. Watching you persevere and grow while enduring one of the hardest police academies in the country made me believe that we can do all things through Christ.

My granddaughter Sophia and grandson Maddox. You are both so special and a complete gift from God! Your smiles and laughter fill a room and bring such joy! You are the beginning of restoration in our family! Love you always, Gramma T.

My cousin Heather Brackenwagon, whom I call HB. Taking care of someone who has cancer takes a special kind of love, and you have that love. I thank God that I was allowed to be a small part of you taking care of that person. Don't ever stop loving people like you did for faith because it is a gift from God!

My cousin Julie Hill, whom I call Jules. Thank you for giving me my first Bible. That act of kindness changed me forever!

My Aunt Ruth Losh, whom I call Aunt Frufie. Your love for people and the way that you make every one of us feel special is such a gift from God! I absolutely love how each of us feels like we are your favorite!

My friend Jennifer Hirt, When I first started to write this book, you came along side of me to help me and you made me believe that I can finish this book! Thank you for believing in me!

My neighbor Rick Bilodeau. You listened to the Lord and came to my house to tell me about how you wrote a book on your phone, which was a confirmation from God that indeed I could do this. Thank you!

MY TESTIMONY

*And everyone who calls on the
name of the Lord will be saved.*

—Acts 2:21 (NIV)

*I tell you that in the same way there
will be more rejoicing in heaven
over one sinner who repents than
over ninety-nine righteous persons
who do not need to repent.*

—Luke 15:7 (NIV)

*They replied, "Believe in the Lord
Jesus, and you will be saved—
you and your household."*

—Acts 16:31 (NIV)

God's Word says in Revelation 12:11, "We overcome by the Blood of the lamb and the word of our testimony." Each of our testimonies are so important to share because it is our testimony that encourages others to know that they have hope to overcome their own struggles. When we speak out our testimony, it helps us to overcome and brings healing to our hearts. As God continues to heal us, our testimonies grow larger and larger. I feel it is so important to write down these stories so that we do not forget the great things God has done in our lives.

The Bible says that the devil comes to steal, kill, and destroy, and that is exactly what he did in my family's life. My life was just a normal, average life until the door of alcohol was opened up, and that's when things really started to change. My dad opened that door, and that alcohol took hold of him and my mom, and it just flooded through our family.

My life became a road of many heartaches and much pain, confusion, and torment. I started drinking at the age of thirteen. By the age of sixteen, I was using hard drugs; by the age of seventeen, I had been arrested for drunk driving and taken to jail. The devil just slowly crept into my family, stealing a little here and a little there until we were all so broken.

When my mother and father divorced, it was so hard to accept because I knew deep down that they really loved each other, but that is what drugs and alcohol do to a family: they divide it. My dad and three brothers moved to New Mexico, and my life slowly slipped farther and farther out of control. I wanted something to be stable and normal in my life. I wanted someone to love me, but I was looking in all the wrong places. By about the age of eighteen, I had gotten pregnant, and because of my drug use and abuse of alcohol, I aborted the baby. If there were ever anything I could take back, it would be that decision, that moment, and that day.

Not long after this, I fell in love with someone I had known for a long time. We got married and had a little girl. This would become the longest stretch of sobriety for me since I started drinking (ten months long), but as soon as she was born, I went right back to numbing the pain inside of me. My marriage started to fail, and within two years, the marriage ended in divorce. I became a master at hiding this brokenness, but all the while inside I was slowly dying. I wanted so badly to be able to control my addiction to alcohol, but it had full control over my life. It was this vicious cycle that just kept repeating itself. So many times, I tried to quit drinking, and I would make it for a few months, but then those thoughts would come. You can have just one drink—everyone does it—you're not the only one who gets drunk—look around you. It was that all-too-convincing voice of Satan dragging me right back into the pit.

By the age of twenty-nine, I had lost my dad, and then three years later, I lost my oldest brother, Patrick, on Mother's Day. I went with my husband to see his mom, and that afternoon, when we returned, we found out my brother had passed away. As the shock started to wear away, I felt so broken and so angry. As I think back to that time, I realize that this is when a part of me really just broke. I just did not care about myself or anyone, and I dove further into my own addiction of alcohol and drugs. I was in another relationship (with the man who is now my husband), and I loved him and my daughter, but now they were on the receiving end of this brokenness and anger that filled me. I cannot tell you how many times I wished to die because at that point in my life I believed that when you die, that was it: no heaven, no hell—just no more pain. I am sure there are so many lost people out there right now who think just like I used to think.

Another eight years would pass by, but this was a time when God started to plant seeds in me, and he used my cousin Lori to plant those seeds. For seven long years, she testified to me little things about God and about the things He did in her life. My mom gave me books to read about the rapture and talked endlessly about these great books she had been reading, and those seeds then started to take some small root inside of me.

I remember so clearly the day Lori called me and asked me to go to church. It was a Wednesday night. I had only been to church one time in my life, and I was thirty-eight years old. I remember feeling physically sick at the thought of going. There was a very real war going on for my soul, and I was clueless about it at that point. But there was this still, small voice inside of me saying, "Go; just go." I got ready to go meet my cousin and her family, and when I arrived, they were all waiting for me. I decided to drive separately, thinking I might not be able to go in, and if that happened, I wanted a way of escape.

As we pulled in, all I could see was the enormous size of the church. I felt so unworthy, so pathetic, and so dirty, like they would be able to see everything inside of me. As I write this and think back to that moment, I understand all too well that we have a real enemy working against us at all times to steal the freedom that Jesus paid a very high cost for us to have.

We sat toward the back of the church. I cannot tell you one word of what Pastor Owens spoke about that night, but I can tell you that at the end of his service, he asked if there was anyone in the congregation who wanted to give his or her life to Jesus, and if so, to please come to the front. My uncle looked over at me and asked, "Do you want to go up?"

I said, "Yes, if you go with me." So my uncle walked me to the front of that church, where I got down on my knees and gave my life to Jesus. While the pastor prayed over me, many in the congregation had come forward, laying their hands over me, and when I went to stand up, they started grabbing me and hugging me. I have never to this day experienced such love from complete strangers.

As I drove out the long driveway leaving the church, I started to cry. I had no idea what it even meant to give your life to Jesus at that time. All I knew is that something happened in that church and something happened inside of me. What I realize today is that the Good Shepherd is always looking for His lost sheep, and He never stops looking. He will go to great lengths to draw you in and show you this love.

One of my most favorite parts of the story about the prodigal son (Luke 15:11–32 NIV) is when the son is coming home and the father sees him off in the distance. He does not stand and wait for the son to reach him. No, he starts running toward the son. I imagine the father grabbing his son and drawing him into a hug that lifts him off the ground! That is how God met me that night I gave my life to Jesus. He used those people in that church to grab me and hug me in a way I had never been hugged yet in a way that was so familiar, like they had known me forever. That night is when my journey began. It is still going to this day and will continue until the Lord brings me home.

I don't know why the Lord chose to save me that night, but I am so glad He did! Thank you, Jesus, for my salvation and for the salvation of every person who may read this. I pray and ask you, Lord, to help us to walk this walk with you.

In Jesus's name,
Amen

Jesus is "'the stone you builders rejected, which has become the cornerstone.' Salvation is found in no one else, for there is no other name under heaven given to mankind by which we must be saved."

—Acts 4:11–12 (NIV)

DELIVERANCE

For the word of God is alive and active.
Sharper than any double-edged sword,
it penetrates even to dividing soul and
spirit, joints and marrow; it judges the
thoughts and attitudes of the heart.

—Hebrews 4:12 (NIV)

I will never forget the first thing God spoke to me: it was the numbers 33 and 3. I heard them all day long, and as I was nearing the end of the day still hearing these numbers, I decided to type them into my computer, and a literal sign popped up:

> **"Jeremiah 33:3 KJV:**
> **Call unto me and I will answer you and show you great and mighty things."**

As I go back to this day, I remember how emotional I felt. I was crying because at that very moment I realized that God had just spoken to me. It is truly amazing how God can take the very simplest thing and use that to speak to His children. Sometimes

He may use people, pictures, animals, books, scripture, and of course the Holy Spirit. Whatever way the Lord chooses to speak to you, it is undeniable in your heart. You just know. But on that day, He chose to use the numbers 33:3—"His Word"—to speak to me, and still to this day, most often He will use His Word to reach me. I love how pure, perfect, and different God's love is for each of us.

At that moment, I wanted to read more, but I had no Bible and was actually too embarrassed to buy one! That seems so unreal to me now, looking back almost eleven years later. The Lord knows all, and He knew this also, so he so graciously had one of my cousins, Julie, give me a Bible.

Deliverance can be a slow process or it can be an immediate process. In my case it was pretty immediate. As I started to read the Word of God, I devoured it. Three years the Lord anchored me to Him. Within a year I was delivered from alcohol, and within two years, all drugs. The only things I did that were different were to give my life to Jesus and start reading the Word of God. I had started drinking at the age of thirteen, and God delivered me at the age of forty. I am now nearing fifty, so it has been ten years that I have been clean and sober. It was not by my power or my might that this was possible; it was by the Spirit of God.

The Bible says in Psalms 107:20 that God sent forth His Word, and it heals us and rescues us from the pit of destruction. Ephesians 6:12 says, "For we wrestle not against flesh and blood, but against principalities, against powers, against the rulers of the darkness of this world, against spiritual wickedness in high *places*" (KJV). When I read these words, the spirit of God came upon me, and I knew at that very moment that I had a real enemy—one who had been stealing from me for a very long time! The Lord then led me to John 10:10: "The thief comes only to steal and kill and destroy; I have come that they may have life, and have it to the full" (NIV).

Jesus came so that I may have life! Not only life but life in abundance! So anything less than this is not from God, and for so long the enemy had been stealing my life little by little. What we must realize is that the devil comes like a thief and takes a little bit here and a little bit there. First, he stole my identity. I lost sight of who I was because pride, rebellion, and bondage had become strongholds in my life. He then took little pieces of my heart by using others to hurt me. My heart became hard; I turned to things to numb me because I just did not want to feel anything anymore. He took the lives of those around me who were indulging in drugs or alcohol, which then opened the door for depression. When I used alcohol, I did things I wished I could forget or take back, but the fact is you can never take those things back. This vicious cycle was my life in a very short paragraph. I could not pull out of the pit I was in until I gave my life to Jesus. It is the Truth that sets us free, and Jesus came to set the captives free!

Deliverance is all through the Bible in both the Old Testament (Exodus 3:8, 6:6) and New Testament (James 5:16; Romans 6:14–19; John 8:32). We see all through the Old Testament the mighty hand of God delivering His people from the evil that is trying to hold them back from the life God wants for them.

The Old Testament is a symbolic representation of the deliverance of sin. It is a temporal deliverance. It is not until Christ Jesus comes that we have complete deliverance, to be free from sin and the grave. For it is by the Blood of Jesus, in His name, and by the Word and the Holy Spirit that we have the power to overcome the evil one. It is called grace. Grace is the unmerited, undeserved favor of God, but it is also the power of God to help you turn away from sin.

When God delivered me from alcohol, he simply removed the desire to drink. It was as if I had never drunk a day in my life. I no longer thought about alcohol, nor did I feel like I wanted to drink. But one must understand that I still had to make a decision: Was I going to drink or not? I still had a free will and a choice to make. Every—and I mean every—stronghold that forms in our life first starts with a thought! It is so important to take your thoughts captive: if they do not align with God's Word, then we are to cast down those thoughts and remind ourselves of what God says in His Word. My whole life had revolved around alcohol—it was the most familiar thing in my life. The hard part was not giving up alcohol; it was learning how to live a different life and learning who I was without it. This is when you must really know who you are in Christ. As I searched out the scriptures I found this list that Joyce Meyer put out there about who we are in Christ. Here are a few of those scriptures:

Who I am in Christ:

I am alive with Christ. (Ephesians 2:5)
I am far from oppression, and fear does not come near me. (Isaiah 54:14)
I have the mind of Christ. (1 Corinthians 2:16; Philippians 2:5)
I am God's workmanship, created in Christ unto good works. (Ephesians 2:10)
I am a new creature in Christ. (2 Corinthians 5:17)
I am a spirit being alive to God. (Romans 6:11; 1 Thessalonians 5:23)
I am a joint heir with Christ. (Romans 8:17)
I am redeemed from the curse of sin, sickness, poverty, and the law. (Deuteronomy 28:15–68; Galatians 3:13)

I am raised up with Christ and seated in heavenly places. (Ephesians 2:6; Colossians 2:12)
I am greatly loved by God. (Romans 1:7; Ephesians 2:4; Colossians 3:12; 1 Thessalonians 1:4)

I will never claim that this was an easy process. I stayed very close to God and leaned on Him at all times. If you are struggling with alcohol, drugs, or some other kind of bondage, I want you to know that God loves you and that God is no respecter of persons—meaning that if He delivered me, He will also set you free. You are important! You matter and your life matters! The Lord chose you and has a good plan for your life!

Failing does not make you a failure. The only person who fails is the one who quits trying. I have found that it is through my failures and trials when I have learned to lean on God and trust in His great love and plan for me. Let your failures be the platform for the great victory that is just around the corner. Let God take your failures and turn them for the good!

Lord, I thank you for delivering me from alcohol and drugs, and I give you all the glory! I pray that you would help whoever may be reading this right now to have the freedom and victory that you paid for them to have. May you bless them and keep them in all your ways!

In Jesus's name,

Amen

So, if the Son sets you free, you will be free indeed!

—John 8:36 (NIV)

It is for freedom that Christ has set us free. Stand firm, then, and do not let yourselves be burdened again by a yoke of slavery.

—Galatians 5:1 (NIV)

MY DREAM ABOUT HELL

Then they cried unto the LORD *in*
their trouble, [and] he delivered
them out of their distress

—*Psalms 107:6 (NIV)*

For great is your love toward me; you
have delivered me from the depths,
from the realm of the dead.

—*Psalm 86:13 (NIV)*

As the Lord started delivering me from the bonds that held me down for so long, I started having dreams. Dreams are strange things: some of them seem to have no real meaning to us, some are funny, some are just odd, some are warnings, and some are terrifying.

As believers in Christ we are to "test the spirits to see whether they are from God." This same command is brought to our attention in other scriptures also. Such as, in 1 Thessalonians 5:20-21 (ESV) we read about Paul telling the Christians to not "despise prophecies, but test everything; hold fast what is good."

And also in 1 John 4:1(ESV) Beloved, do not believe every spirit, but test the spirits to see whether they are from God, for many false prophets have gone out into the world"

One of the dreams that I had was about hell. I had this dream at least ten years ago now, and I have never forgotten it. I wished at times I could forget it because it was terrifying, but to this day I can remember almost every detail. I know that this dream may be disturbing to some, probably because we want to believe in our hearts there can be no such place as hell. We are so desensitized to hell from the movies, music, and video games that we see and hear that I believe many people today think like I used to think—that there is no such place. Maybe that is why the Lord allowed me to see it with my own eyes, so that others can know that it is real. I don't know for sure, but I do know that I saw it and that as I searched out Gods word I truly believe what I saw was real.

I drove by this particular sod field all my life growing up; it was about five miles from my house. In my dream it seemed as though the sod field I saw was this same field. As I walked out across the field, a round porthole opened up in the ground. I remember looking down the hole, and as I did, I heard a child crying—not just any child, but my own child. Panic started to rise up in me, and I started to go down into the hole; there were rungs to go down the shaft. It was pitch black, and the farther I went down, the louder I could hear the cry.

As I started to descend, suddenly there was a small amount of light, and as I looked forward, the light shone in front of me, and I saw the most grotesque monsters. They were huge, and each was in its own cage with chains on the legs and arms—they were part human and part monster. As they saw me coming down, they tried to swipe at me, but the chains held them in place. Terror is about the only word I can use to describe what I was feeling and seeing, but as I continued to hear the cry of a child that sounded like my own, I went further and further down.

The shaft turned into tunnels, so I began to crawl on my belly through more tunnels. It seemed that I would never find the place where the crying was coming from. The whole time, as I crawled on my belly, I could hear people screaming hysterically at me, "GET OUT! GET OUT!" I could not see the people, but somehow they knew that I was down there.

I came to an opening and saw a cage with a small child in it, and as I looked, I could see that the child's eyes and mouth were stapled shut, and there was a monster (demon) in the cage with the child guarding it. I was hysterical and started screaming, "GIVE ME THE KEY!" and as I was screaming, all I could hear was people screaming back at me, "GET OUT! GET

OUT!" They were pleading with me to run! I knew that something big was coming for me—but I was not leaving until I had the key to free this child.

Suddenly I turned and looked behind me and saw a pair of eyes looking at me through the slats in these wooden boards. I pleaded with these eyes to give me the key, and the person slid me the key through the opening in the boards, I somehow knew that he/she was going to be tortured for it. I turned and stuck the key in the lock, and as soon as I turned the lock to open the door, I was pulled up through the tunnel at the speed of light and sat straight up in my bed. I just sat in my bed for some time trying to get a grasp on what had just happened to me. I began to calm down and then thought, What was that? I really had no idea what I had just experienced. All I knew was that it seemed so real and so completely terrifying.

Not long after my dream, my friend Sheila called to tell me about a book she wanted me to get called *23 Minutes in Hell.* I did not like scary books and really did not want to read it, but over the next few months, she continued to tell me about the book. At this time, I still did not know what my dream was about. I had not forgotten it, but I was just chalking it up to a very scary experience. So, as my friend persisted in my reading this book, I decided to go and get it. I stayed up all night reading it. As I finished this book, there was absolutely no doubt in my mind that what I saw was hell! I was terrified as I went back over my dream. I was terrified for my family and friends because some had not given their lives to Jesus, and the thought of one person I know going there threw me into terror. For one week, I cried uncontrollably. I could not stop crying for the people I heard screaming. I finally could not take this weight; I felt that it was crushing my soul. It really was like I was back in the dream and experiencing it all over again. I prayed to God to please take it away, and the Lord removed everything (depression, grief, sorrow, heaviness, oppression) from me except the actual dream.

Now we come to the why. Why did God allow or want me to see this? As I started to really seek the Lord about this dream, I was driving one day and I heard the Holy Spirit say to me, "It was you down in that cage." (This was as I was driving to pick up a prescription that I was addicted to.) And then I heard Him say, "You did not love yourself enough to go down." I knew what the Spirit was saying to me because I still had so much shame and hate for myself. I did not love myself enough to care if I died or lived but there was one person whom I did love enough to go down for and that was my daughter.

I have since come to believe that God had two reasons for allowing this dream:

1. I had an open door. I was still in bondage, and I believe that God wanted me to see what it looks like when we are in bondage. I had one foot in the kingdom and one foot in hell. God never left me and had no intentions on giving me up, but we all have a free will, and I was seeking God and asking Him to help me with this addiction I had to prescription pills.

2. I also believe that the Lord allowed this dream because I did not really want to believe that hell was real, and I had not gotten to scriptures that really taught about hell.

This experience has changed me forever. I know that there is a heaven and there is a hell. I know that some people will believe this and some will not. My job is not to make you believe. I am just telling my story because I believe God wants me to tell it. There is a question that the Holy Spirit asked me one day much later after my dream. He said, "What would Jesus be saving you from if there was no hell?" You see, some people get confused about hell. Hell is simply being separated from God. God is everything good in this world: He is love, joy, peace, patience, kindness, goodness, faithfulness, gentleness, meekness, and long-suffering (Fruit of the spirit; Galatians 5:22 KJV). Hell has none of these things: it is total darkness, fearfulness, torment, suffering, and complete terror.

As I continued to seek God about my dream, these are some of the scriptures He led me to:

"I will give you the keys of the kingdom of heaven; whatever you bind on earth will be bound in heaven, and whatever you loose on earth will be loosed in heaven" (Matthew 16:19 NIV). Remember, I was screaming for the key—the key that would set me free. Well, God gave me that key as He led me in His Word. That key is Jesus.

"Be strong and courageous. Do not be afraid or terrified because of them, for the LORD your God goes with you; he will never leave you nor forsake you" (Deuteronomy 31:6 NIV). I had already given my life to Jesus when I had this dream, and God's Word says He will never leave us nor forsake us.

"Again Jesus spoke to them, saying, 'I am the light of the world. Whoever follows me will not walk in darkness, but will have the light of life'" (John 8:12 ESV). The little amount of light I was seeing was the Holy Spirit going down with me—it was the only light down there.

"And I remind you of the angels who did not stay within the limits of authority God gave them but left the place where they belonged. God has kept them securely chained in prisons of darkness, waiting for the great day of judgment" (Jude 1:6 NLT). The monsters that I saw in the cages: I do believe this is what the book of Jude is talking about.

I like to think of myself as a person who believes without seeing, but I know all too well I must be more like doubting Thomas, who had to see to believe. This is what love does: it chases after us and will go to great lengths to show us this love. Perfect love casts out all fear. God is Love and satan is fear.

Lord, I thank you for delivering me out of the pit of hell and showing me the truth about my own condition. I pray that if we are being deceived in any way, you would expose it and help us to overcome those things that try to hold us down. I thank you, Holy Spirit, for never leaving us nor forsaking us. It is true that no man on earth nor devil in hell can take us out of the Father's hand.

In Jesus's name,
Amen

MY BROTHER ALEX SAW HEAVEN

*In the last days, God says, I will pour
out my Spirit on all people. Your
sons and daughters will prophesy,
your young men will see visions,
your old men will dream dreams.*

—*Acts 2:17 (NIV)*

I remember the morning my brother Alex called me to tell me about his dream. Most times he had night terrors, so when he was happy and excited to tell me about his dream, I was excited to hear about it. One of the things I loved most about Alex was his great enthusiasm! He said it was the best dream he ever had, and he tried so hard to go back to sleep. As he started to describe the dream, he said he was in a place with white pillars, and he was sitting at a table, and sitting across the table was me, our cousin Lori, and my friend Sheila. Sitting next to Alex, he said, was Jesus.

Of course, I pummeled Alex with questions. Did He talk to you? What did He look like? Could you see Jesus's face? To these he replied that, no, he did not see His face, and he did not know how he knew it was Jesus; he said he just knew. He said Jesus got up from the table and came back with wine and was serving us wine. He said it was so real and the most amazing feeling he had ever felt in his life. He actually described it as the best high he had ever felt. He mentioned several times how clear we all looked to him and that it was like he could touch us. He said he never wanted to leave, and when he woke he tried so hard to go back to sleep. But the most amazing part of the dream was that he could still taste the wine on his lips when he woke up and that it was like nothing he had ever tasted before.

My first thought was, Why were we across the table? I kept thinking about him saying to me, "You were so clear, I could see you perfectly." I don't know if Al ever told anyone else about his dream, but I did not forget it.

Months went by, and my brother got into some trouble where he ended up in jail. We prayed for him and put him on prayer chains all over the country, and months later he was released into a Christian rehab where he would end up saving a man's life, and then he himself would be baptized. He was still struggling with his addictions but was staying clean. It was getting close to his release date, and I started thinking about his dream. God tells us to test all spirits, so I started to look in the Word of God about his dream, and I came across this story in Luke 22:26–30 (NLT):

> Those who are the greatest among you should take the lowest rank, and the leader should be like a servant. [In Alex's dream, Jesus was serving us wine.] Who is more important, the one who sits at the table or the one who serves? The one who sits at the table, of course. But not here! [on earth] For I am among you as one who serves [the Holy Spirit in us] "You have stayed with me in my time of trial. And just as my Father has granted me a Kingdom, I now grant you the right to eat and drink at my table in my Kingdom. [The Holy Spirit was revealing what was to come: Alex was sitting *right* next to Jesus in his dream (I believe he was given a vision of heaven to come) and Lori, Sheila, and I were across the table (we are still here on earth).]

When I found this word, I knew that my brother had a very real encounter with Jesus, but I still thought about why was he next to Jesus and we were across the table, and what did it mean?

My brother was released from rehab and about ten days later became very ill with MRSA. He would go on to battle MRSA for about a month but ended up losing this battle on August 16, 2008. I was so grieved from this loss in my life. There were so many things I just did not understand at that time. My heart still cries as I write this story because I miss my brother.

But as I started to seek God about Alex, the Lord kept leading me back to the dream that He gave him. I believe in my heart God gave Alex a glimpse of heaven, of what was to come in his life. You see, he was sitting next to Jesus (in heaven) and we were across the table (here on earth). Maybe the dream was more for me than him, a sign of God telling me He has my brother—Alex is at the table where the greatest feast ever will take place when we have all arrived back home. He also let me know that where Alex is, it's a place you will never want to leave, a place of joy like we have never experienced here on earth!

Approximately two days before Alex passed away, I was reading a book called *And The Angels Were Silent* by Max Lucado.

The last sentence of the book was **"See you at the table."**

Thank you, Lord, for giving Alex this dream! This has brought such peace to me, and I am thankful that my brother shared it with me. My prayer is that if others are suffering, wondering if heaven is real, they would know it really is real. There really is a place filled with such great love that all darkness falls away and will never enter. We really are meeting in heaven for the greatest feast ever!

See you at the table, Al.

Love,

Sis

The master will dress himself to serve and tell the servants to sit at the table, and he will serve them.

—Luke 12:37 (NCV)

SITTING QUIETLY WITH GOD

If you declare with your mouth,
"Jesus is Lord," and believe in your
heart that God raised him from
the dead, you will be saved.

—Romans 10.9

We were learning how to sit quietly with God at church, to listen instead of talk. What is God saying to you? As I sat in my prayer chair, silence fell over me, and I sat waiting to hear what God had to say to me. I was used to telling God everything or asking for everything, so waiting for God was something different for me.

As I sat in my chair, a vision came to me, one I was very familiar with. It was of my brother Patrick the night before he passed away. We were at my mom's house, and she had made pork chops for dinner. I remember that because my brother inspected each and every pork chop like he was with the USDA. I remember my cousin Lori and me laughing about it.

The vision was of him standing in the doorway of the bathroom. Patrick was holding a book, pointing at a picture in the book, and saying this is real, and he continued to say over and over that he believed it was real. When he brought the picture over for me to look at it, I noticed the book was very old, and it had gold picture plates taped into it. The picture he was looking at when he came to show me was a picture of Jesus on the cross. I remember looking at it, thinking, Yup, that's Jesus. I was not yet saved, or I had not yet given my life to Jesus at this point. I thought it was weird he was making such a big deal about these pictures and this book he was reading.

My brother Patrick has been gone now for seventeen years. This experience I am now writing about happened about four years ago—this vision of me seeing my brother in the doorway had been coming to me for thirteen years! As I sat quietly with God, I finally asked Him why I was seeing this vision and what it meant. It never occurred to me to ask God about it until that very moment. The very minute I asked God, these words came to me: "If you confess with your mouth and believe in your heart, you will be saved!"

Suddenly revelation came over me: my brother was confessing with his mouth and believing in his heart ALL night long! Then I remembered I still had the book and had never looked at it to see exactly what my brother was reading. I ran to get the book, and as I started looking through the pages, I saw that every one of them had pictures of saints, and at the bottom of each page there was scripture: "GOD's WORD," which is sharper than a double-edged sword piercing the soul and dividing soul and spirit. This word penetrated my brother and a spirit of truth came upon him.

I sat in my chair in complete amazement, crying at the love and mercy of God

Two days later I went to my mom's house to help her plant flowers and do some gardening. We went in to take a break and get something to drink. As we sat down, I thought about my experience with God. I was not going to say anything, but as I sat with my mom, I felt like telling her about it. As I shared with her everything that God had revealed, she got wide eyed and started to cry. "What is it?" I said.

She said, "Tammy, you are not going to believe this! Two days ago I looked at Patrick's picture and asked God for a sign that he made it to heaven!" At the exact moment when I was sitting in my chair quietly with God, my mom was asking God for a sign: "Did my son make it to heaven, Lord?" Here I came with her sign my brother made it! I had no idea how tormented my mom had been after losing her son as to whether he had gone to heaven or not, but God almighty knew, and on that day in my mom's living room peace came flooding in, and we sat crying and laughing. God showed up!

Whatever you need answers to, God is the one you turn to. He will give you the answer, but you have to be looking for it. So many times, we miss it because we will not be still and look for God. The Lord *loves* to reveal Himself. That is part of having a relationship, and for me it is the best part.

These are a few of the scriptures God led me to while writing this:

"He says, 'Be still, and know that I am God'" (Psalm 46:10 NIV).

"Listen! The Lord's arm is not too weak to save you nor is his ear too deaf to hear you call" (Isaiah 59.1NLT).

[I will hear your prayers] In those days when you pray, I will listen. (Jeremiah 29:12 NLT).

DON'T LOOK BACK

But Lot's wife looked back as she
was following behind him, and
she turned into a pillar of salt.

—Genesis 19:26 (NLT)

Grief can be an all-consuming thing that will drag you down into the lowest of pits. As I get ready to write this story, I am grieving the loss of my mom. My heart feels so sad and I miss hearing her voice so badly that it feels like my heart could break at times. It is very normal to grieve. Jesus himself grieved when His friend Lazarus died.

This grief I am feeling right now is different than the grief I felt at the loss of my youngest brother, Alex. I had regrets about my brother and guilt for leaving him at the hospital. I had been staying at the hospital for about two weeks, and Alex started to improve, so I decided to fly back home. I went to tell my brother I was leaving, and he begged me not to go, but I assured him I was coming back. I was going home for a while then coming back with Mom. There was this small voice inside telling me not to go, but I knew I was coming back, so I went anyway. After I'd been home for about a week, my brother started to worsen, so my mom and I started to drive back to New Mexico, but as we were about halfway there, we got the call that Alex had passed away.

I was grief stricken, hysterical, and so angry at myself for leaving. Depression covered me like a blanket, and I probably cried every day for a year. I went over and over everything in my head. God, why did you have me anoint his head and pray for healing over him? Why did you save him only to let him die? Why did I leave? Why did he have to die? Why did he have to suffer so much? Why, why, why? I replayed over and over the day I left when Alex said, "Don't go," and I assured him I was coming back, but I was too late. I started to doubt God's love for me, and these negative thoughts consumed me. These thoughts were of course from the enemy. God tells us to cast down thoughts and imaginations that try to exalt themselves against God's Word. This means that if a thought does not line up with what God says, then it is a lie from the pit of hell. I was meditating on negative thoughts, and I was being consumed with a spirit of grief. God never stops loving us and never leaves us.

One day as I was walking, I heard so clearly the Holy Spirit say, "Don't look back." That's it—just three words. Then the Lord led me in His Word to the scripture about Lott and his wife running out of Sodom and Gomorrah. In the scripture when Lott's wife looks back, she turns to a pillar of salt. Now every day as I walked, I heard the same thing: "Don't look back." I knew what God was saying if I continued to look back at this event in my life— if I continued to hold onto my guilt and pain—I too was going to remain frozen in time, never to move forward in my walk with God. But as soon as I would try to move on, the grief and the pain and the wondering why I left would rush back and stomp all over the thought of letting go.

Then, one day, I received a letter from a prisoner. I was a writer for one of the local churches and used to write to prisoners. This prisoner knew nothing about my personal life, but God would use this prisoner to speak directly to me. In the letter, he wrote and told me, "Don't look back," and gave me the very scripture about Lott and his wife running out of Sodom and Gomorrah. As I sat staring at this piece of paper, this all-consuming grief broke inside of me, and all I could do was sob. This was the moment when I really started to understand how much God loves us—as the scripture says, no one knows the depth, the length, the width, or height of God's love; it is too big. On that day, I got to see to what length the Lord will go to show us this love.

I remember this day like it was yesterday. It was seven years ago. I have let go of my little brother. He is in heaven, where there is no pain or suffering. Most of all I have forgiven myself and allowed God to heal me. I know that there are so many out there who are broken from the loss of losing someone, and maybe you had or have guilt, anger, or regrets about the tragedy of losing that person. First, I am so sorry for your pain, and second, please try to let God love you and heal you. I promise if you seek the Lord, He will show up and this most tender love will heal you.

Don't look back. Let God heal you; he loves you so much.

The LORD is close to the brokenhearted and saves those who are crushed in spirit.

—Psalms 34.18 (NIV)

He heals the brokenhearted and binds up their wounds.

—Psalms 147:3 (NIV)

HERE I AM; I WILL GO

Jesus said to them again, "Peace to you! As the Father has sent Me, I also send you."

John 20:21 (NASB)

God desires to use us to touch the lives of others, and we do not need to go to far-off places to do this. It happens at our jobs, at our neighborhoods, at the store, at the gas station, in church, in meetings, on vacations, and in our everyday living. There is a scripture that comes to mind as I get ready to write this story: "Then I heard the voice of the Lord saying, 'Whom shall I send? And who will go for us?' And I said, 'Here am I. Send me!'" (Isaiah 6:8 NIV).

I remember when I first read this passage, I was a baby in Christ, and the first thing I said was, "Send me; I'll go." So fearless, until God sends you—then so terrifying! Whoever says, "God is boring" has probably never done the things God calls each of us to say or do! As you read the Bible, you will see for yourself that God had people do some things that we just don't understand while reading the story, but as we get to the end of the story, we get to look back and see the great plan God had all along. I love it!

I was struggling in my business, so I started to pray for a part-time job. I had not even had time to look, and my sister-in-law called and asked if I needed a job. Umm, yes, I just prayed to God for one! It was a job cleaning for a sorority up at MSU. I had worked in an office for the last ten years and did not really have experience with professional cleaning, but I needed this job. As a matter of fact, Sharon, who hired me, said she knew as soon as she spoke to me, before she ever met me, she was going to hire me. This job has been one of the greatest blessings in my life looking back eight years later. God has used this job and the people I work with to heal my heart from the many losses in my life and deliver me from pride, haughtiness, fear, and so much more. The Lord has filled me with humility, trust, and love. What I have learned is that God will use the position you are in to build character, integrity, humility, love, patience, and so many other things needed to do God's work and to bring healing to our hearts. I once heard a pastor say, "We must first be a servant before we can ever be a leader." Over these last eight years, I have used this time to listen to God and let

Him fill me with His love, wisdom, understanding, and discernment.

Moving along in this journey: after being in this housekeeping position for about three years, I started praying God would open another door of opportunity so I could make more money. I had shut down my business, so my only income was my part-time cleaning job at the sorority. A friend I had not seen in maybe ten years contacted me, and as we talked, I mentioned to her that I was looking for more work. Weeks later she sent me a text about a job at a school. I contacted the school, they set up a time for an interview, and a few days later they called to hire me for the position. The Lord will and can provide for you in so many ways, and in this incident, He used someone whom I had not seen in ten years to tell me about a job opportunity!

It was a door opened by God, and I realized this, so I prayed, "God, if there is anyone you want me to pray for at this school, please bring them forward." Not long after I started, a little girl by the name of Grace (name has been changed) came to my cleaning cart each day. She was about five, loved to ask questions, and was so smart. After some time of Grace visiting me, I knew she was the one to pray for. Months went by, and I did not discern anything with her; she seemed so happy—but we all know how resilient children can be.

During this time, I was leading a bible study about "offense." It was a John Bevere Study called

"The Bait of Satan." What a great study! It was teaching us how to not be easily offended. During this time in this new position there was someone in a authoritative position, who was a Christian, and this person was offending me. I felt like this person looked down on me. This person would not acknowledge me as we passed each other in the hallways and would not wave in parking lots, and I started to feel very disrespected. In short, I wanted to leave this job because I was "offended"—the very topic I was teaching on. Remember, God opened the door for this job. I knew God had led me to pray for this little girl, but I had no idea why. Now I was offended, and my first thought was, "I don't make enough money to deal with this!" This is exactly how the devil moves you out of a position when God is trying to teach you something or use you for the Kingdom. I could leave, but if I was really allowing God to work in my life, I knew I would get another test just like it.

I had been at this job for over six months when I finally saw the mother of the little girl I was praying for. She was heading into the after-school program room. She was about five feet eleven and looked like she weighed about ninety pounds. I had no idea if this really was Gracie's mom, but this was what I was thinking the Holy Spirit was revealing to me as she walked by. I was pushing my cleaning cart about to go into the elevator, but also trying to wait and not make it obvious, because I wanted to see if she came out with Grace but the elevator door closed. I was in the elevator, and my first thought was, "She is a drug addict—that's why God has me praying for Grace." The Holy Spirit immediately convicted my heart because I had no idea if she was or not; all I know was that I believed God was telling me it was the young girl's mom. So I started praying for Gracie's mom.

A few more months went by, and during this time I was still being persecuted by offense. I still wanted to leave this job, but I continued to stay and pray for these two individuals. My cousin Heather called me, and she informed me she was coming to the school where I work to pick up a little girl she was going to be watching. I asked her what the little girl's name was, and she told me Grace. I was a little bit shocked and told her I had been praying for a little girl named Grace and to send me a picture when she picked her up so I could see if it was the same little girl. As soon as she arrived, she sent over the picture, and *yes*, it was the same little girl. She told me her mom (the one I thought was a drug addict) was very sick with cancer. My cousin had taken care of her years before but had lost track of them. But the mom, Faith (name also changed), called the hospital one day and by chance got my aunt, who works on the switchboard and is my cousin Heather's grandmother. Faith asked if my aunt knew how to get in touch with Heather.

So then my cousin began to take care of this child and mother whom the Lord had had me praying for. What are the chances of this happening by accident? Zero! No chance. This is how the Lord operates: there is no such thing as a coincidence. I do not believe in coincidence at all. I do believe that with every job the Lord gives us there is *always* a purpose for us.

As Heather started to care for Faith and Gracie, she reported to me at how very sick the mom was. I asked Heather if she would let us come and pray for her, but she was too afraid to ask her, so we waited for the door of opportunity to open. As months went by, I was sensing in my spirit an urgency to pray for Faith. I continued to ask God for the opportunity to pray for her.

Then one day, as I was leaving work, I looked and noticed that my car was the only one in the parking lot except for truck parked so close to my car that it appeared to be touching it. As I was walking toward my car, I was thinking, Who in the world would park like this? There was a whole parking lot! As I got to my car, around the end of the truck came Faith— yes, Gracie's mom. She was holding onto her truck to steady herself. I passed by her and said, "Hi." I got into my car, and as I sat and watched Faith make her way across the parking lot to get her little girl, I broke down. My heart was just hurting for this mom.

She was so frail, so weak, but she refused to give up on life and the basic things we all take for granted, such as picking up her little girl at school.

I was also crying because I was terrified—because I knew God wanted me to pray for her, and she did not even know me. I was a complete stranger! I was now trying to negotiate with God about this. "Lord, I cannot do this; she is going to think I am crazy! What do I say?" My heart was pounding from fear! I looked up, and there she was, coming toward me with little Grace in tow. I had to do this—I had been praying for the opportunity for months!

I stepped out to meet her at the back of my car. I said hi to Gracie and extended my hand and said hi to Faith. I said, "You don't know me, but my cousin Heather has been taking care of Gracie, and I want you to know I have been praying for you." She was so humble and so meek. She smiled and said thank you. I told her that if she ever wanted us to come and pray with her, we could come to her house. Then the Holy Spirit prompted me to ask her if I could pray for her right there in the parking lot. She said yes, I could, and that she had been waiting for someone to come. Right there, all alone in the parking lot of the school, we prayed together. I cannot tell you exactly what I prayed because at that moment the Holy Spirit took over. After we finished, I told her that God loved her, and we parted ways.

I called my cousin crying. It was such a moment of love and peace that God completely set in motion. I went on to meet Faith four more times: two times at her house, once when Heather had to call an ambulance for her, and another time when I went to check on her and ended up just sitting with her having apple pie. The third time I met her at the hospital, where I asked her if she believed in Jesus, to which she replied yes. The last time I saw Faith was in hospice, where Faith lost her fight with cancer.

I went to her funeral, and when I saw a picture of her before she got sick, I was shocked at how it seemed cancer had stolen her beauty. But that was a lie—her beauty was still there because beauty can never be stolen; it is on the inside of us. When she died, I was so sad I thought God had sent me there to pray for healing in her body. I wanted God to heal her, but God's plans are not always aligned with what we want. He sees a bigger picture that we cannot see. So I asked God why he sent me. It was such a simple response. I felt as though He said He wanted Faith to know He loved her, and He used me and my cousin to show her that love.

Remember how offended I was at the beginning of this job? So many times, I wanted to leave but did not feel that God was releasing me from this job. I stopped talking about the person who was offending me and started praying for him (which we learned in our Bible study, and also the Lord spoke to me and told me to quit talking about this person and pray for him) and the offense was broken. This person actually went so far as to make me a card and give me a bonus, telling me what a great job I was doing! Was this for real? God does not want us looking to people for approval, because if you seek the approval of people, then you will always be easily moved out of the position God is trying to use you in. I doubt this person ever knew how offended I was. I truly think that Satan was just using him to move me from this position. Prayer is one of the most powerful weapons we have as a Christian, and I have seen God move mountains by the power of prayer.

After the funeral, I put in my two weeks' notice (I had gotten a new job at the homeless shelter), and while I was downstairs cleaning, Gracie came to see me to tell me she was moving in two weeks.

Thank you, Lord, for using me and teaching me so much at this job. Thank you for showing me that most often when you send us to pray for someone, it is about us showing your love to that person. Yes, God uses us to heal, give words of wisdom, and lead others in salvation, but most of the time, we are going for the simple act of love.

God is love.

—1 John 4:8 (NIV)

OVERCOMING FEAR

*Yea, though I walk through the valley
of the shadow of death, I will fear
no evil: for thou art with me; thy rod
and thy staff they comfort me.*

—Psalms 23:4 (KJV)

In 2 Timothy 1:7, Paul writes, "God did not give us a spirit of fear but one of power, love and a sound mind (NKJV)." One of the things I noticed about this scripture is that God first gives us power, then love, and then a sound mind—because it is the power of God's word and the Blood of Christ that fear has to flee. The Word of God says submit yourself unto God, resist the devil, and he will flee! Fear is the opposite of faith, so it is always opposing us in every part of our life.

One of my greatest fears was public speaking—so much so that I did not finish my associate's degree because of a speech class that was required. After I gave my life to Jesus and the Lord started to use me in different ways, there always came these moments when I would need to speak in front of others. Slowly God placed me in these positions, and with each situation, I became a little more confident. For example, I joined a Bible study, where we would have to talk about our study or things we were going through. We started a prayer group, which opened the door to pray out loud with my prayer partners. I took a part-time job at the homeless shelter, and I would have to stand up and give announcements; then at night I would have to gather the women, and we would all hold hands and I would pray over all of us.

God then opened the door for me to go into the prisons with my cousin Lori and her best friend, Mary Jo. When I started going, I went in as a prayer intercessor, but gradually the Holy Spirit started to gently talk to me about giving my testimony. For three years my cousin would ask me, "Tootie (that is what she calls me), do you want to give your testimony this time?" Always I would look at her and say, "Noooo..." For three years I said no. Remember me saying to God, "Here I am; I will go"? I was terrified—literally terrified—to stand up and tell these women about my life. But the Holy Spirit kept on gently nudging me. I tried everything to convince myself that I did not need to do this, but I knew that I did in fact need to do this because I was being held in bondage to fear, and if I did not do this, it was going to hold me back from other things God would want me to do.

So, on the way down to our next visit at the prison, my cousin looked over at me and asked the question, "Tootie, do you want to give your testimony today?" I said, "Yes, I do." She yelled and cheered as we continued to drive. I was paralyzed with fear, and I had no idea how it was going to happen, but it was going to happen. My cousin was now preaching in the auditorium, so there were probably between eighty and a hundred women. I got up to talk and felt like my whole body was shaking. I was overcome by a spirit of fear so powerful I could barely talk. I had written down my testimony—thank God, or I would have never said a word. The first thing God had me say was 2 Tim 1:7: "God did not give [me] a spirit of fear but one of power, love and a sound mind." Then the Lord had me speak another scripture: "[We overcome] by the blood of the lamb and the word of our testimony (Revelation 12:11 KJV)." That word spoken bound the fear, and I was able to speak, but it was not a pretty sight. I cried uncontrollably to the point where the women I was supposed to be lifting up were consoling me! I was a mess! And the women were yelling, "It's okay! You can do it!" And I did. I made it through, and this congregation of beautiful women stood and cheered for me! I will remember that day for the rest of my life!

The spirit of fear was broken off of me that day. However, that does not mean I do not ever feel fear; it just means that if I do, I do what I need to do afraid, with and by the power of God. I am writing this four years later, and now, as we look back at that moment, we just laugh because we were supposed to be going in to encourage these women, but in fact, God used them and still does use them to encourage us.

What I have learned most is that we are all a part of the body of Christ, and just as God uses us to speak to those women, He also uses them to speak to us. We are all in this walk together. When one part of the body is broken, we as believers are to rally around that brokenness with prayer and love. Every part of the body is important.

Thank you, Lord, for helping me to overcome fear. May you also help the people reading this to know that they too can be free from every kind of fear that may be holding them back in their life.

In Jesus's name,
Amen

So do not fear, for I am with you; do not be dismayed, for I am your God. I will strengthen you and help you; I will uphold you with my righteous right hand.

—Isaiah 41:10 (NIV)

There is no fear in love. But perfect love drives out fear, because fear has to do with punishment. The one who fears is not made perfect in love.

—1 John 4:18 (NIV)

GREATLY LOVED BY GOD

*Blessed are the pure in heart
for they will see God.*

—Matthew 5:8 (NIV)

This one is for you, Mom. I love you!

Last year I had a dream that I was in an airplane, flying along just fine, and then suddenly the airplane started to veer into a building. The wing of the plane clipped a high-rise building, and I remember feeling panic, thinking I was going to die. The next thing I knew, I was drowning in the ocean, and as I screamed for Jesus to help me, I looked right through the clear water, and I could see the arm of Jesus reaching down from heaven to grab me. Jesus never left heaven, nor did I see His face. The next thing I knew, I was in an apartment with some people, and I was trying to tell them that Jesus saved me. It seemed like they could not hear me or just did not believe me—I couldn't tell which, but I remember I was persistent in trying to tell them. Then I woke up from the dream. I did not really seek God about this dream, but I kept thinking about it. Not long after my dream, the Lord led me to the scripture:

> "Blessed are the pure in heart for they will see God" (Matthew 5:8 NIV).

Another week went by. I went to pick up my mom to go to lunch, and she wanted to stop at Rite Aid. My mom loved to shop at Rite Aid! And there were times I had to go in to round her up because she could be in there for over an hour. She assured me she was just running in, so I waited and waited and waited. Probably forty-five minutes later, my mom came out. I will tell you I was irritated and started to say, "*Mom*, what have you been doing?"

She said, "Oh, shopping," and then she was excited to tell me she bought me something. She got in the front seat and pulled out a pedestal made out of plaster that had a book opened up on the top, on which was written the scripture, "Blessed are the pure in heart for they shall see God."

Let me just say two things about when God repeats himself:

(1) it means something, and (2) take note.

I thought, "Okay, God, you have my attention. You are trying to tell me something."

About two months later, my mom became sick, and we discovered she had small-cell lung cancer. As the doctor said those words, "Judy, you have cancer," we both started to cry, and so did the doctor, who loved my mom. We went to the doctor thinking my mom had pneumonia and left in complete shock.

We then got in my car and drove in complete silence. I was crying so hard on the inside, but I did not want to scare my mom. I wanted to scream out in hysterics, "NOOOOOOO," but I kept silent. I finally looked at my mom and told her they had no idea if she really had cancer. "Who knows? It could be that stupid sponge they left in you after your surgery." My mom laughed, but I knew she was scared. My mom decided against treatment because it was too advanced, and within three months, she was gone.

I almost did not include this story because it is so raw and painful still. But God went to great lengths showing his love for my mom and also showing me that He has full control. I do not know why my mom had to go home to be with the Lord so quickly, but I trust God. Once again, I know that God sees the bigger-picture things we cannot see.

After the celebration of her life, I received many cards. One card came from my cousin Kelly Jean, who lives up north. Taped to the front was a picture of a sunset over the water with my mom's face superimposed coming out of the water. I opened the card and set it by my prayer chair, and about two days later, I saw the scripture on the front of the card: "Blessed are the pure in heart for they will see God!" I asked Kelly Jean if the Lord led her to put that scripture on the front of the card. She said yes, that actually she had a different scripture on the front of the card, and the Lord had her change it to "Blessed are the pure in heart for they shall see God."

Just before my mom passed away, I wanted to ask her to ask God to send me a sign when she got to heaven. But I did not want the devil to hear my request, so I never asked her. Instead I asked God inside my head to send four rainbows. The funny thing is when I asked God this, I thought, "I know this is going to be hard," only because I had never seen four rainbows at one time. This is actually pretty funny, considering I am asking the creator of the whole universe to send me four little rainbows and thinking it would be hard. At first I looked every day for these rainbows and saw nothing—not even one rainbow.

Then in June of this year, we took my mom's ashes out to New Mexico to put her by her sons, who are also out in New Mexico. It was nearing the eight-month mark of her being gone. I had quit looking for rainbows; I was too caught up in my sadness of having

to leave my mom's ashes 1,700 miles away. I had never been that far away from her—not for forty-nine years, that is. We had a beautiful service for her with all our family out west, and soon it was time to head back home. After driving about seven hours, we were getting close to leaving New Mexico and heading into Texas. We were about ten minutes before entering Texas, and it started to rain. As it started to rain, we started to see rainbows off in the distance. Before we left the state of New Mexico, we saw eight rainbows! I was staring in complete amazement at the faithfulness and love of our Lord. No, He did not give me one rainbow nor even four rainbows, but He gave me eight rainbows! Rainbows were chasing us as we left New Mexico, seemingly riding right above us. I think God gave me one rainbow for every month my mom had been gone.

"Is anything too hard for the LORD?" (Genesis 18:14 NIV).

I believe that my dream represents everything that I went through with my mom. I was flying along just fine, and then suddenly my life veered off, and this large crash happened. The same is true of my mom: her life was going along just fine, and on one normal day, the doctor came out and told my mom she had cancer. It felt like I was drowning, and I am sure it felt the same for my mom. But God heard our cry for my mom, and I believe that his arm ever so gently reached from heaven and saved her from the depth of that ocean of fear. I absolutely love the card that God had my cousin send me because my mom is out of the water, the water is calm, and she is smiling. This is how I imagine it was as she entered heaven. And now I know why God gave me that dream, because no matter what we are facing in life, we have a Savior, and His name is Jesus. He will reach deep into the depths to save us. When we cry out to Him, he hears us. Jesus is our redeemer.

"Blessed are the pure in heart for they will see God."

Thank you, Jesus!

Love always,

Tammy J. Glenn

IN CLOSING

If you have never given your life to Jesus and would like to, the first step is to invite Him into your life. The next step is to start reading your Bible. I remember a sermon I heard where the pastor said that the book of John was written so that a man might believe. I think that is a good place to start. Find a church or prayer group to attend. Let God's Word heal you. It is by the power of the Holy Spirit and the Word that you will find healing so that you too will begin to share your testimony.

These stories are true events that have happened in my life. They are my testimony, and there are so many more. As I said in the beginning of this book, your testimony is so important, not only for you but for others to hear. And the last thing I would like to say is don't give up! The devil is going to work so hard to make you believe this is not real and that you cannot overcome whatever it is you are going through. But I am here to tell you different: you are an overcomer! Greater is He who lives inside of you than he who lives in this world! You matter! Your life matters! If you need help, reach out. Do not isolate yourself—that is a tactic of the enemy!

May God bless you and keep you always! In Jesus's name, I pray.

PRAYER OF SALVATION

P ray this prayer out loud:

Lord Jesus, I repent of my sins against you and ask you to come into my heart, mind, body, soul, and spirit and be my Lord and Savior. I believe you died for my sins and rose on the third day and you are now seated at the right hand of the Father. I ask you to fill me with your Holy Spirit and help me on this journey. I ask you to fill my life with your love, your wisdom and your understanding.

Thank you for not giving up on me and for saving me.

In Jesus's name,
Amen

If you have given your life to Jesus, I would love to hear from you, or if you simply have questions, please email me at Savedbyjesus2018@gmail.com.